旋轉的頭巾

The Swirling Hijaab

Na'ima bint Robert
Nilesh Mistry

Chinese Translation by Sylvia Denham

mantra lingua

我媽媽的頭巾是黑色，柔軟而且寬闊，

My mum's hijaab is black and soft
and wide,

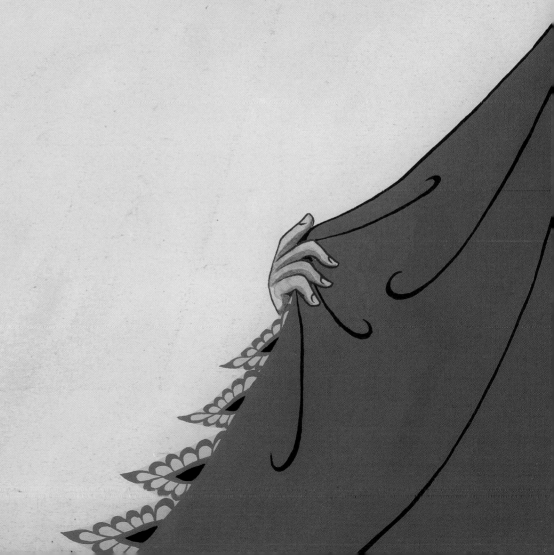

一個讓我躲藏在裏面的堡壘！

A fort for me to hide inside!

船上在空中拍動著的風帆，

A ship's sails flapping in the air,

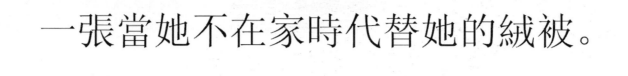

一張當她不在家時代替她的絨被。

A comforter when she's not there.

一個遊牧民的帳篷，

A bedouin tent,

一件嫁衣披紗，

A wedding sari,

我的茶聚用的臺布。

A cloth for my tea party.

一位戰士女王的斗蓬，

A warrior queen's cloak,

一個遊牧民的行李包袱，

A nomad's baggage,

當我需要休息時的毛氈！

A blanket when I need a rest!

但包蓋著我的媽媽
作爲她的信仰的一部份
是頭巾的最佳用途。

But covering my mum
as part of her faith
Is what the hijaab does best.

Bismillahir-Rahmanir-Raheem

For the daughters of Islam; past, present and future

N.B.R.

For Saarah, Farheen & Rayaan

N.M.

The Swirling Hijaab is one of many sound enabled books.
Touch the circle with TalkingPEN for a list of the other titles.

First published in 2002 Mantra Lingua Ltd
Global House, 303 Ballards Lane, London N12 8NP
www.mantralingua.com

Text copyright © 2002 Na'ima bint Robert
Illustrations copyright © 2002 Nilesh Mistry
Dual language text copyright © 2002 Mantra Lingua
Audio copyright © 2008 Mantra Lingua
All rights reserved

A CIP record for this book is available from the British Library